BEN
the bulldog

DAISY
the dachshund

ROVER
the mongrel

MR. CHIPS
the black Labrador

HENRY
the Pekingese

WENDY
the other mongrel

To Leon Achilleos
P.H.

To Jimmy Wool
B.F.

Text copyright © 1993 by Peter Hansard
Illustrations copyright © 1993 by Barbara Firth

First U.S. edition 1994
First published in Great Britain in 1993 by
Walker Books Ltd., London.

Library of Congress Cataloging-in-Publication Data

Hansard, Peter.
Wag, wag, wag / by Peter Hansard ; illustrated by Barbara Firth.
—1st U.S. ed.
Summary: Pictures labeled with words such as sniff, woof,
chase, leap, splash, shake, dig, gobble, and sleep present the
afternoon adventures of several lively dogs.
ISBN 1-56402-301-X
[1. Dogs—Fiction.]   I. Firth, Barbara, ill.   II. Title.
PZ7.H19822Wag   1994
[E]—dc20   93-3536

10 9 8 7 6 5 4 3 2 1

Printed in Italy

The pictures in this book were done in pencil and watercolor.

Candlewick Press
2067 Massachusetts Avenue
Cambridge, Massachusetts 02140

WAG WAG WAG

Peter Hansard

illustrated by
Barbara Firth

CANDLEWICK PRESS
CAMBRIDGE, MASSACHUSETTS

sniff   sniff

roll   piddle

drool

dribble

woof

woof woof   play ball

chase

race

pant

leap

splash   shake

dig   dig

scratch
scratch
scratch

walk   sit

yawn

tug

nip   chew

gobble   gobble

gnaw

sleep

snore

wag wag wag

K-3

HONEY the yellow La...
and her puppies

The cat

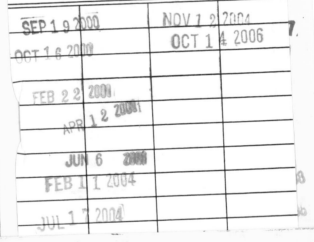

JO-JO
the Jack Russell terrier

th... ...orkshire terrier

SUSIE
the West Highland terrier